30 SECOND MYSTERIES

FOR KIDS

Editorial Director: Erin Conley

Designers: Lynn Gustafson, Jeanette Miller and Lisa Yordy

Special thanks to Suzanne Cracraft, Lynn Gustafson, Audrey Haworth,
Emily Jocson, Jennifer Ko, Cris Lehman, Maria Llull, Tami Sartor, Lani Stackel
and Rosie Slattery for their invaluable assistance!

30 Second Mysteries, Spinner Books and The Book You Can Play! are all trademarks
of University Games. Copyright © 2004 by University Games Corporation, San Francisco,
CA 94110. All Rights Reserved. No part of this book may be used or reproduced in any
manner whatsoever without the written permission of the Publisher. University Games
Europe B.V., Australiëlaan 52, 6199 AA Maastricht Airport, Netherlands. University Games
Australia, 10 Apollo Street, Warriewood, Australia 2102.
Retain this information for future reference

Printed in China.

ISBN 1-57528-919-9

CONTENTS

INTRODUCTION

Each 30 Second Mystery is a fun, interactive form of a good old-fashioned whodunit. This new collection of cases promises to entertain you, your friends and family for hours, and is sure to exercise your noggin. I had a great time putting these mysteries together and hope that you have even more fun trying to solve them.

We are already working on more mysteries for the 30 Second Mysteries series and would love your help. Write your own case with four clues and submit it to me through my publisher, University Games. If we include it in the next edition, we will list your name as a contributor in the credits and you can truly be part of the story.

Good luck!

— Bob Moog

RULES

OBJECT

To be the first player or team to solve 7 mysteries or score 7 points.

PLAYING THE GAME

First things first: grab a pen and paper to keep track of your points.

- The youngest player spins first to determine the type of mystery to be solved (i.e. Who, What, Where or Why) and reads the first Case and Mystery from that category out loud to the group. This player acts solely as a reader and may not play until the mystery is solved. The player to the left of the Reader gets the first clue—and the first stab at solving the mystery.

- If a player guesses the mystery incorrectly (or doesn't have a guess), the player to his/her left gets the next clue and may then try to crack the case. Play proceeds in a clockwise fashion.

- If a player guesses the mystery correctly, s/he earns a point and the player to the Reader's left becomes the new Reader for the next case in the same category. Do not spin again until each player has read a mystery to the group.

- Once all players have acted as the Reader, it is time to spin again! The player to the left of the last person to spin now spins to determine the type of mystery to be solved. S/he is the first reader for this round.

- *Tip:* Don't forget to jot down the number of the last mystery solved in case you spin the same category more than once—which is likely to happen.

SCORING

First player to guess the mystery scores 1 point. If a player solves the mystery without hearing any clues, s/he earns 2 points.

WINNING THE GAME

The first player to score 7 points wins!

PLAYING ON YOUR OWN

Spin and read the Case and Mystery topic question from the appropriate category. Cover clues with a bookmark. Try to solve the Case after revealing each clue.

SCORING

- 4 points = 1 clue revealed
- 3 points = 2 clues revealed
- 2 points = 3 clues revealed
- 1 points = 4 clues revealed
- 0 points = Incorrect guess!

WINNING THE GAME ON YOUR OWN

Read 10 mysteries. Collect 20 points or more and you're a winner!

Who?

BAWLING BALDIE

A bald male opens his eyes and finds himself naked in a small room full of people he doesn't recognize. A female grabs him and starts to slap him before he can say anything. The male is shocked and bursts into tears.

THE MYSTERY

Who is the male and who is the female?

THE CLUES

The male is not being punished.

The female went to school to learn to treat the male this way.

The male weighs less than 10 pounds.

The male and female are in the hospital.

CASE 1 SOLUTION

The male is a baby and the female is a doctor (obstetrician).

Who?

THE STRANGE STRANGER

A famous stranger bursts into a house where two children named Conrad and Sally wait alone for their mother. He tries to make the children play games they don't want to play. Eventually the stranger leaves, but the police are not called.

THE MYSTERY

Who is the stranger and who made him famous?

THE CLUES

The stranger is wearing a hat, gloves, a bow tie and a fur coat.

A famous Doctor brought him to life, but the stranger is not real.

The stranger's friends are two Things.

The stranger is a cat.

CASE 2 SOLUTION

The stranger is the Cat in the Hat. Dr. Seuss made him famous.

Who?

MURDER AND TRICKERY

A man finds himself surrounded by mean strangers who want to eat him. He runs away, only to encounter fierce animals and other problems. Finally, he places his trust in a friendly stranger, only to be tricked and murdered.

THE MYSTERY

Who is the man and who tricked him?

THE CLUES

The man can't swim, but the stranger can.

The man is irresistibly sweet.

The man tells everyone he can run faster than they can.

The friendly stranger has a very foxy mind.

CASE 3 SOLUTION

The man is the Gingerbread Man, who was eaten by the fox.

Who?

A FATHER ALONE

A father lovingly cares for his baby after its mother has left them. He gives up his own comfort for many months while he protects the child from danger. Finally, the mother comes back and the father immediately goes off to sea, leaving his little one behind.

THE MYSTERY

Who is this father?

THE CLUES

Without the father, the child would die almost instantly.

The father knew the mother was coming back.

The father lives with many other fathers in Antarctica.

The father wears only a tuxedo but he is not human.

CASE 4 SOLUTION

The father is a penguin.

Who?

BODY DOUBLE?

On her 16th birthday, Taylor goes to the DMV to get her driver's license. The clerk tells Taylor that earlier that same day another girl with the same birth date, last name and address also got a driver's license. The clerk asks Taylor if she is a twin and she truthfully answers that she is not.

THE MYSTERY

Who was the other girl and how is she related to Taylor?

THE CLUES

Taylor knows the other girl very well.

Taylor and her brother celebrate all their birthdays together.

When Taylor was born, her family was on the news.

Taylor's mother knitted three baby blankets during her pregnancy.

CASE 5 SOLUTION

The other girl is Taylor's sister, but they are triplets, not twins.

Who?

THE BRAVE LADY IN THE NIGHT

In the dark of night during the Civil War, a daring woman performed feats that few would even think of. Over many years, she put herself and others in harm's way with her shocking adventures, but in the end she escaped unharmed. After meeting her, people were never the same again.

THE MYSTERY

Who was this person and what is she famous for?

THE CLUES

People think of the woman as a great American heroine.

She did her best work in the 1850s and 1860s.

She helped countless people make a safe passage.

She traveled on a "railroad."

CASE 6 SOLUTION

Harriet Tubman is famous for helping to free slaves on the Underground Railroad.

Who?

THE STRANGER IN THE NIGHT

A woman steals into Kelly's room at night, intent on taking at least one thing with her when she leaves. Kelly is not aware of this visitor, but would not be afraid if he knew she was there. The woman and Kelly have never met.

THE MYSTERY

Who is this woman and what does she leave?

CLUES

The items the woman takes from Kelly are not valuable.

Kelly is six years old.

The woman's visit is profitable for Kelly.

The woman is not a witch, but she's not human either.

CASE 7 SOLUTION

The woman is the tooth fairy.
She leaves small sums of money.

Who?

STALKER OR NOT?

In downtown Paris, only a thin pane of glass separates an unknown man and a famous woman. The man stares at the woman for nearly three hours. Rather than get annoyed, the woman simply smiles back at him.

THE MYSTERY

Who is the woman?

THE CLUES

The woman has no eyebrows.

The woman looks good for her age, which is about 500.

The man is at the Louvre Museum.

The woman was created by the famous painter Leonardo da Vinci.

CASE 8 SOLUTION

The man is looking at the
Mona Lisa.

Who?

THE VANISHING MAN

One man's image has inspired many songs, stories and poems. Some have even traveled record-breaking distances to visit him. For as long as anyone can remember, people have seen him every night. However, he only shows his face from a distance; when people get close, he disappears.

THE MYSTERY

Who is this man and what part of him are people able to see?

THE CLUES

He is surrounded by stars, but he's not an actor.

Some people think that he has an unlimited supply of green cheese.

He shows himself when it gets dark out.

People first visited his home in 1969.

CASE 9 SOLUTION

He is the Man in the Moon, whose face people see when gazing into space.

Who?

THE VOLUNTEER WITH A SECRET

A man keeps responding to emergencies, even though he is not a police officer or firefighter. He provides his own uniform and performs these good deeds without ever being paid.

THE MYSTERY

Who is the man and what is printed on his uniform?

THE CLUES

The man changes into his uniform in many different places.

The man is a reporter.

The man's uniform is blue—and it's very tight.

The man can leap tall buildings in a single bound.

CASE 10 SOLUTION

---

*The man's name is Clark Kent (or Superman)
and there is an "S" on his uniform.*

Who?

THE PUZZLING PATRIOT

An American patriot traveled on a small horse to a faraway village. When he arrived, he placed part of a bird into his clothing. He then did something very strange, announcing to everyone that he some Italian pasta with him.

THE MYSTERY

Who is the patriot, and what is the Italian pasta?

CLUES

The first part of the patriot's name tells you he's from the North, not the South.

His small horse was a pony.

Most people learn about the patriot in a song.

He put a feather in his cap.

CASE 11 SOLUTION

*The patriot is Yankee Doodle Dandy and
the pasta is macaroni.*

THE UNIQUE TEACHER

Jessica's foreign language teacher is never absent and is always in a good mood. She even takes Jessica and a bunch of other kids on a field trip every single day of the week. They all practice their foreign language skills while learning how to read a map and stay away from foxes.

THE MYSTERY

Who is Jessica's teacher and what language does she teach?

THE CLUES

The teacher always brings a backpack.

They often visit the teacher's Abuela.

The teacher has her own TV show.

The teacher is a child.

CASE 12 SOLUTION

Jessica's teacher is Dora the Explorer.
She teaches Spanish.

Who?

A FEARLESS FELLOW

Every day of his life, a fellow faces danger, often finding himself staring at the barrel of a gun. His superior mind allows him to escape every time, usually by poking fun at others. When it's all over, he goes to bed underground.

THE MYSTERY

Who is this rascal?

THE CLUES

Despite his name, he is not an insect.

Kids have enjoyed him for generations.

His favorite food is carrots.

His favorite catchphrase is, "What's up, Doc?"

CASE 13 SOLUTION

He's Bugs Bunny.

Who?

MURDER FOR HIRE

Christina is a contract killer, but strangely enough, the police are not interested in arresting her. She is always invited into the very homes where her murders will take place, and her work is done in front of witnesses. No one even tries to stop the killings.

THE MYSTERY

Who is Christina and how does she kill her victims?

THE CLUES

Christina never uses a gun to kill.

After a year on the job, she's likely killed thousands, maybe even millions.

Christina usually has to wear a mask when she is working.

Christina hates pests.

CASE 14 SOLUTION

Christina is a professional exterminator.
She poisons her victims.

Who?

THE CEMETERY SPEECH

In wartime, a tall man gives a moving speech at a Pennsylvania cemetery. People are sad for the dead, but the man's words make them feel better. Even though he only speaks for about two minutes, the man's words remain important through many generations.

THE MYSTERY

Who gave this speech and what was it called?

CLUES

The speech took place during the Civil War.

This man was the president, and he was later assassinated.

The speech starts with these words: "Fourscore and seven years ago..."

He gave the speech for the men lost in a famous battle.

CASE 15 SOLUTION

President Lincoln gave the famous speech,
called the "Gettysburg Address."

Who?

UNSEEN SAM

Sam has lived in the United States all of his life. He likes the military but doesn't like wars. He works for the government but isn't in politics. Everyone feels they are related to him, but no one has actually ever met him.

THE MYSTERY

Who is Sam?

THE CLUES

He started working during World War I and has been working ever since.

He is always seen on posters pointing at people and telling them, "I Want You…"

He has white hair and a beard and he always wears a hat.

He represents patriotism.

CASE 16 SOLUTION

He is Uncle Sam.

Who?

THE CASE

While taking a midnight stroll, Kareem is viciously attacked. After quickly rubbing something all over his body, the attackers go off into the night. The attackers didn't have weapons, but Kareem has definitely lost some blood.

THE MYSTERY

Who was attacking Kareem and what drove them away?

THE CLUES

Kareem killed a few of the attackers with his bare hands.

The protection Kareem used was a lotion.

The attackers are very small and hard to see at night.

His attackers didn't kick or punch, but they did a lot of biting.

CASE 17 SOLUTION

Kareem was bitten by mosquitoes.
They stayed away after he applied insect repellent.

Who?

THE SECRET GANG LEADER

Out on a boat on a foggy night, a gang of teenagers lands on an island that's said to be filled with phantoms and ghosts. Ignoring the spooky islanders, this gang unmasks the villains, gets back in its van and continues on its merry way, roaming the country to solve crimes of all kinds.

THE MYSTERY

Who is the shortest member of this gang?

THE CLUES

It's almost impossible to understand what the shortest gang member is saying.

He's only short because he walks on four legs.

He'll do anything for a snack.

His best pal is Shaggy.

CASE 18 SOLUTION

The shortest member of this gang
is Scooby Doo.

What?

CASE 1

WHO WAS THAT MASKED MAN?

A masked guard is attacked by a gang of five men who shoot at him, then quickly flee. He survives the attack, but the gang returns again and again for 60 minutes before it quits. The next night, a different gang attacks him. The gangs never use guns.

THE MYSTERY

What is the masked man's profession?

THE CLUES

The man is very goal-oriented.

The man and his attackers are all wearing uniforms.

The man is in front of a net.

The man is wearing ice skates.

CASE 1 SOLUTION

The masked man is a hockey goalie.

What?

THE AMAZING ESCAPE

A famous man in handcuffs stands on a bridge surrounded by a large group of people. Suddenly, the man leaps off the bridge into the cold, fast-moving river below. Oddly, he does not drown but climbs out of the river safe and sound and is met by an applauding crowd.

THE MYSTERY

What is the man's name and why did he leap into the river wearing handcuffs?

THE CLUES

The people watching knew that the man was going to jump into the river.

The man was a famous magician.

The man died in 1926.

The man's last name rhymes with "meanie."

CASE 2 SOLUTION

The man was Harry Houdini, who leapt into the river as part of his show business act.

What?

CASE 3

THE LITTLE THIEF

The young son of a single mother leaves home to trespass on his neighbor's property. While there, he steals from the neighbor and takes off all his clothes before running back home. Although he is seen and chased, he is not caught and no charges are pressed.

THE MYSTERY

What is the son's name and whose property does he steal?

THE CLUES

The son has three sisters.

He has large ears and wears only a blue jacket and clogs.

The neighbor doesn't like this little thief in his garden.

The son was created by Beatrix Potter.

CASE 3 SOLUTION

The son is Peter Rabbit, and he steals
Mr. McGregor's vegetables.

ROUND AND ROUND

Each working day, Celia seems to run in circles to get things done. Instead of becoming frustrated by doing things over and over, she seems to love it. As she sees it, speed is her friend—and the faster she gets through her work, the better.

THE MYSTERY

What is Celia's job and why doesn't she mind it?

THE CLUES

To do her job well, Celia really has to put her foot down.

If things get out of control where Celia works, someone could get hurt.

Timing is everything in her line of work.

Her work outfit includes a helmet and a jumpsuit.

CASE 4 SOLUTION

Celia is a racecar driver who loves circling the track.

What?

THE FREQUENT FLIER

Zoe travels all over the world for free without ever buying a plane ticket or paying for a hotel. She travels quickly-in some cases she visits three different continents in a single week. She works in every country that she visits, but only gets paid in one.

THE MYSTERY

What is Zoe's occupation and what type of company does she work for?

THE CLUES

The company Zoe works for requires its employees to wear uniforms.

Zoe has really taken off in her career.

Zoe doesn't stay long in any one place.

Zoe has wings pinned on her uniform.

CASE 5 SOLUTION

*Zoe is a pilot who works
for an airline.*

What?

THE UNCAGED CREATURE

A man captures a wild animal and brings it back to civilization. When left alone, the animal often gets into trouble and the man must set things right. Luckily, when the animal looks for the man, his special clothing makes him easy to spot.

THE MYSTERY

What special clothing does the man wear and what is the animal's name?

THE CLUES

The animal's first name is an adjective that also means "inquisitive."

The man always wears a hat.

You can read about the animal in books.

The animal likes to monkey around.

CASE 6 SOLUTION

The man always wears a big yellow hat;
the animal is Curious George.

What?

THE UNUSUAL HERD

A group of men takes care of a large number of horses. People come from miles around to watch them. The horses run all day and into the night, stopping only for short breaks. The men never feed the horses, even though they are their sole source of income.

THE MYSTERY

What type of horses are they?

THE CLUES

The horses never stray far from their home and always follow the same path.

The horses have endured for many years.

Riding the horses can have its ups and downs.

The horses travel in circles.

CASE 7 SOLUTION

The horses are
carousel horses.

What?

IT'S A TOUGH JOB, BUT ...

Todd puts on makeup and a strange outfit to prepare for work. His job makes some people laugh, but those he works with just want to kill him. Though Todd always wears crazy clothes, he really only wants one individual to pay attention to him while he's working.

THE MYSTERY

What does Todd do for a living and whose attention does he want?

THE CLUES

Todd often uses a barrel in his work.

Todd works with animals, but they're not trained to do tricks.

Todd doesn't work in Hollywood, but he still deals with a lot of bull.

Todd gets a lot dustier than most clowns.

CASE 8 SOLUTION

Todd works as a rodeo clown who tries to distract the bull from the fallen rider.

What?

AUSTIN'S ODD OCCUPATION

Austin is a government worker who spends his whole day sitting down. Customers pay money and then watch him sit. Austin ignores these customers while he looks outside his office window. If Austin does his job right, the customers leave as soon as he is finished.

THE MYSTERY

What is Austin's job?

THE CLUES

Austin wears a uniform while he works.

Unless it's a very busy day, the customers stay seated while they are with Austin.

When the customers leave Austin they are on the street.

Austin is driving a vehicle.

CASE 9 SOLUTION

Austin is a bus driver.

What?

CASE 10

THE UNUSUAL EXPLOSIONS

Mary straps her son Nicholas into a machine and then casually turns it on. After a series of explosions, Mary turns off the machine, unstraps Nicholas and leaves the machine behind. Neither Mary, Nicholas, nor the machine are harmed.

THE MYSTERY

What type of machine is this?

THE CLUES

Mary owns the machine.

The explosions are mechanically controlled and are perfectly normal.

Mary needs a hand-held tool to get into the machine and to turn it on.

The machine was made by Ford.

CASE 10 SOLUTION

The machine is a car. (The small explosions in the engine are what make it run.)

What?

A WEIRD CAREER

Sara must be very careful coming and going from her workplace each day, because it can be very dangerous. Once at work, she sits all alone in the same spot and stares out the window. She does not change her position much during the day—but change is a big part of her job.

THE MYSTERY

What is Sara's job?

CLUES

The view from Sara's window changes all the time.

People give her money all day, but she cannot spend it.

People roll down their windows to talk to Sara.

She works at a bridge, but she might want to transfer to a turnpike someday.

CASE 11 SOLUTION

Sara is a tollbooth collector.

What?

THE LOST LETTER

Brandon asks Aisha for her address to send her a letter. Aisha checks the mail every-day but the letter never comes. She later finds out that Brandon was involved in a crash and could not get the letter to her. Brandon is not injured and there is no damage to his car.

THE MYSTERY

What happened to Brandon, and whose fault was it?

CLUES

Aisha received all of her other mail.

The address Aisha gave Brandon did not include a zip code.

The crash happened at Brandon's desk and it didn't make any noise.

Aisha's address had the word "yahoo" in it.

CASE 12 SOLUTION

Brandon had Aisha's email address and his computer crashed. It was no one's fault.

What?

UNPARKED PARKER

Parker travels over 200 miles in a day, yet he is home for dinner every night. He rarely sees the same people from one day to the next, but he is almost never alone. He stops his vehicle often, but Parker rarely parks.

THE MYSTERY

What is Parker doing and what color is his vehicle?

THE CLUES

Parker works in a big city.

Parker is not afraid to use his horn.

Parker charges by the mile.

Parker drives a car with a sign on the top.

CASE 13 SOLUTION

Parker is driving a taxi;
his vehicle is yellow.

What?

THE PRICE OF FAME

The stars of a TV show are upset that they were chosen. They will probably not be on the next episode or, if they are, it will be their last appearance. They do not audition for the show—they are chosen by the producers to be seen by America.

THE MYSTERY

What is this TV show?

THE CLUES

The audience doesn't vote, but the producers hope they'll call in.

The host of the show continually asks America for its help.

The show is nonfiction. All the characters are real.

The show helps the FBI catch criminals.

CASE 14 SOLUTION

The show is
America's Most Wanted.

What?

IS CURTIS CRAZY?

Curtis carries a book of matches in his pocket. Every night, he walks into a room full of people, takes out the book of matches and amazes every person in the crowd. Curtis hears gasps, sighs and then applause, but he can't speak while the audience is reacting.

THE MYSTERY

What is Curtis's profession?

THE CLUES

It's likely that no one else in the crowd can do what Curtis can.

Curtis's mouth is full while he works.

Curtis is an entertainer and his act is hot stuff.

Curtis is carefully trained in pyrotechnics.

CASE 15 SOLUTION

Curtis is a fire-eater.

What?

HARSH JUDGMENT

Michelle slowly slides her fingers against the silver blades in her hand to check their sharpness. Next, she looks in the mirror and prepares to be judged by a group of people from around the world. Michelle will not enter a courtroom, yet the group's judgment may affect both her and her country.

THE MYSTERY

What is Michelle doing?

THE CLUES

Michelle does not walk or talk in front of the group.

She is surrounded by ice, yet Michelle wears very little.

This is Michelle's golden opportunity.

Music plays while Michelle is in front of the group.

CASE 16 SOLUTION

*Michelle is a figure skater competing for
a gold medal.*

What?

A MYSTERIOUS HERO

An entire town watches a man in uniform save hundreds of lives every day. The hero has a special sign that gives him this life-saving power. He is an elderly man with white hair and a slow step, yet he can stop a fast-moving truck with one hand.

THE MYSTERY

What do people call this man and what is the symbol that gives him his power?

THE CLUES

He can stop all kinds of vehicles, but he can't stop a speeding bullet.

Most kids know him well, but he's not in the movies or comic books.

His sign is a red octagon and his uniform is an orange vest.

He works at an intersection.

CASE 17 SOLUTION

The man is a crossing guard who uses a stop sign to control traffic.

What?

CASE 18

THE RECKLESS DRIVER

Thirteen-year-old David drives a car for several hours before tiring. He sees several police officers and often exceeds 100 miles per hour. David never pays for gas and ignores most traffic signs, yet he is not pulled over and he doesn't get a ticket.

THE MYSTERY

What is David doing?

THE CLUES

David and his brother took turns driving.

David crashes the car several times.

The car runs on electricity.

David finally stops the car when his thumbs get tired.

CASE 18 SOLUTION

*David is playing
a video game.*

Where?

BEN THERE, DONE THAT

Ben has a high profile and an easy-to-recognize face. People all over town look up to him. Guards protect his home 24 hours a day, while Ben entertains visitors, poses for pictures and provides a valuable service without any worries at all.

THE MYSTERY

Where does Ben live and what service does he provide?

THE CLUES

Ben depends on his hands and face.

Ben is English.

Ben is not a person.

People expect Ben to always be on time.

CASE 1 SOLUTION

*(Big) Ben tells time
in London.*

Where?

THE CONFOUNDING CORPSE

A man's body is found in California, 1,000 feet below sea level. He's dead, but drowning is not the cause of death. The spot where the man lost his life is well known as a killer place to be.

THE MYSTERY

Where and how did the man die?

THE CLUES

The man was not near the ocean when he died.

Water would have saved the man's life.

The man died in the desert.

The man died in a valley named for its deadly heat.

CASE 2 SOLUTION

*The man died from the heat
in Death Valley.*

WHAT'S CORY'S STORY?

A steady stream of people enter Cory's workplace and remove its treasured belongings. The people do not pay for what they take. Cory allows them to take as much as they want as long as they keep it quiet.

THE MYSTERY

Where does Cory work and what are the people taking?

THE CLUES

Cory is more of a lender than a seller.

Cory works in a public place that is run by the city.

Cory sometimes thinks of his customers as a kind of worm.

Sometimes Cory makes people pay when they bring the belongings back late.

CASE 3 SOLUTION

Cory works for a library; people are taking
(or checking out) books.

WHERE'S WYATT?

Wyatt rides his bike out of a big city. As he travels, he sees water on either side of him and two orange towers above him. After about 15 minutes Wyatt stops, turns around and admires a tall pyramid.

THE MYSTERY

Where has Wyatt stopped?

THE CLUES

It is foggy, but Wyatt can see an old prison on an island in the distance.

On the right side of Wyatt is a bay, on his left is the Pacific Ocean.

Wyatt rode past a tollbooth.

Wyatt is in San Francisco.

CASE 4 SOLUTION

Wyatt has stopped on the
Golden Gate Bridge.

30 SECOND MYSTERIES FOR KIDS
Where?

THE HUGE HOLE

Four reddened people walk to the edge of a hole, where they stop and gaze in. This starts to make them dizzy, so they look out (not down) at the rocks before them. Soon, they climb onto animals and begin their long journey into the hole.

THE MYSTERY

Where are these people?

THE CLUES

The animals are burros.

The people are sunburned because this place gets pretty hot.

The hole is one mile deep and has been a national park since 1919.

It's located in Arizona.

CASE 5 SOLUTION

They are in the Grand Canyon.

30 SECOND MYSTERIES FOR KIDS
Where?

THE FRIGHTENED CAPTIVE

A boy who is all alone is taken to a seat by a woman in uniform. She is a stranger to him, but she straps him to the seat. He cries but is told to be quiet and sit still. Hours later, the boy is freed and is told he may leave. He doubts that he will ever see the woman again.

THE MYSTERY

Where is the boy and who is the woman?

THE CLUES

The woman is just doing her job.

The boy's parents are waiting outside for him when he leaves.

While they are together, the woman feeds him and gives him headphones.

When the boy leaves the woman in uniform, he is in a different city than the one he met her in.

CASE 6 SOLUTION

The boy is on an airplane.
The woman is a flight attendant.

30 SECOND MYSTERIES FOR KIDS

Where?

CASE 7

THE TRIP TO NOWHERE

On a three-day weekend in May, Moss hops into his car in Indiana and begins to drive. He drives for hours in one direction, going hundreds of miles. When Moss stops the car and gets out, he's still in Indiana. In fact, he's in the same place that he started.

THE MYSTERY

Where is Moss?

THE CLUES

Moss drove in this state last year at the same time.

Moss is doing his job.

Moss is in Indiana's capital city.

Moss often drives more than 100 miles per hour without getting a speeding ticket.

CASE 7 SOLUTION

---

*Moss is driving in the
Indianapolis 500.*

THANKS, BUT NO THANKS

A man enters a sweepstakes and is notified by mail that he has won third prize: a new refrigerator. The man has a home, but does not have a fridge. Even though there are no hidden costs and he needs to keep his family's food cold, he turns down the prize.

THE MYSTERY

Where in the US does the man live and what is his home called?

THE CLUES

The man is a fisherman who built his house by himself.

The man's home is white.

The man lives in the largest US state.

The man usually uses snow to keep his food cold.

CASE 8 SOLUTION

---

*The man lives in Alaska
in an igloo.*

JULIO'S HOME

Julio is an American citizen born in 1996. He has never been out of the country, but he has also never entered a single US state. He could easily take the bus to two of them but he just hasn't gotten around to it yet.

THE MYSTERY

Where does Julio live?

THE CLUES

Julio lives on the North American continent.

Julio lives in a capital city.

Julio lives near the Smithsonian Institution and Capitol Hill.

The two states near Julio's house are Virginia and Maryland.

CASE 9 SOLUTION

Julio lives in Washington D.C.

IT CAME FROM UNDERGROUND

The ground beneath a group of unsuspecting people gurgles and groans. Steam escapes from a hole nearby and suddenly a violent sound bursts out, followed by an amazing white-hot display of force. Instead of running for their lives, the people step closer and gaze in wonder.

THE MYSTERY

Where are these people?

CLUES

This display can be seen about once an hour.

It can reach heights of 106–184 feet.

It can be seen in Yellowstone National Park.

In 1870, this natural attraction was named for its reliable performance.

CASE 10 SOLUTION

*They are visiting the
Old Faithful geyser.*

LEADFOOT LYDIA

Hughes Bank has just been robbed! Two miles from the bank, Lydia is racing down the highway. She has not committed a crime, but three police cars are hot on her trail. Lydia does not pull over—and continues to speed through traffic with the police following her every move.

THE MYSTERY

Where is Lydia heading and what is her profession?

THE CLUES

Lydia will continue at top speed until she reaches her destination.

Lydia is not breaking the law and knows the names of all the police officers following her.

Lydia carries a revolver and a club, and she won't hesitate to use them.

Lydia wears a badge.

CASE 11 SOLUTION

Lydia is a police officer heading toward Hughes Bank.

MISERABLE ISABEL?

Every morning before sunrise, Isabel leaves her apartment and goes to sit in a small room all by herself. In the room, she listens to music and talks out loud for four hours. Isabel is alone the whole time, but she is not considered crazy, and she even gets paid for this strange behavior.

THE MYSTERY

Where does Isabel go every night and why is she there?

THE CLUES

The room is occupied 24 hours a day.

Isabel is wearing headphones and the room is sound proof.

Isabel isn't talking to herself.

If the people listening to Isabel want to talk to her, they'll have to call in.

CASE 12 SOLUTION

Isabel is a disc jockey and she is in the room to host her late-night radio show.

WHERE'S CLAIRE?

Claire watches a group of men standing below her. She sees one of the men get caught trying to steal, while another just stands by and does nothing. Suddenly, the people around her stand up, stretch their legs and begin to sing. Claire quickly joins in.

THE MYSTERY

Where is Claire and what does the crowd sing?

THE CLUES

Claire has been sitting in the same place for two hours.

Claire's brother and dad are sitting next to her, and are both wearing the same hats.

Claire ate a hot dog and a box of Cracker Jacks® an hour earlier.

The song includes the words, "Root, root, root for the home team."

CASE 13 SOLUTION

---

*Claire is at a baseball game. The crowd sings
"Take Me Out to the Ball Game."*

WATCH YOUR STEP

Maria takes small, careful steps every night, often using a stick to help her along. Strangers watch her, but no one ever offers to help. The threat of Maria stumbling causes some people to shield their eyes.

THE MYSTERY

Where is Maria working and what is she doing?

THE CLUES

Maria isn't sick or old.

Maria really looks down on her audience.

Flashy outfits make up most of her wardrobe.

Her job requires amazing balance.

CASE 14 SOLUTION

*Maria is at the circus
walking a tightrope.*

30 Second Mysteries for Kids — Where?

THE INTERNATIONAL MAN OF MYSTERY

A man who is known by many different names has an international reputation, but he has never been seen. Occasionally, he dashes out under the cover of night. His home is very remote and nearly impossible to reach.

THE MYSTERY

Where is the man's home and what is he called in the US?

THE CLUES

The man is old, but age doesn't slow him down.

The man usually wears a suit.

The man has never been on a plane, but has flown all over the world.

The man employs little helpers to carry out his business.

CASE 15 SOLUTION

The man lives at the North Pole and he is called Santa Claus.

30 SECOND MYSTERIES FOR KIDS

Where?

CASE 16

LUCKY CHUCK

Chuck spends his time going door to door, performing icky tasks all day. He likes helping people and doesn't mind when he has to go to the hospital. Some people treat him badly, but others are nice; whatever their mood, they all call on him when the going gets tough.

THE MYSTERY

Where does Chuck work and how does he earn his living?

THE CLUES

Chuck really knows people, inside and out.

Emergencies happen every day where Chuck works.

Most of the people Chuck helps are lying down.

A stethoscope hangs around his neck, but Chuck is not a doctor.

CASE 16 SOLUTION

Chuck works at a hospital as a nurse.

30 Second Mysteries FOR KIDS

Where?

THE STRANGE CHAMBER

Erin enters a large building. She is stopped by a man in uniform and is asked to prove her identity or leave the building. Erin is taken to a machine where her belongings are inspected and some items are taken from her. She then eats a sandwich and waits in a high security area until she can leave.

THE MYSTERY

Where is Erin and what is she waiting for?

THE CLUES

The room Erin sits in features lots of chairs and a giant window.

One of the items taken from Erin is a pair of scissors.

Erin is waiting in New York, but she is very worried about reports of a storm in London.

About 10 minutes after she leaves the building, Erin is flying high.

CASE 17 SOLUTION

Erin is at the airport waiting for a flight to London.

30 SECOND MYSTERIES FOR KIDS

Where?

NOT A TYPICAL TRIP

A group of four comes together to follow a road they believe will cure all their problems. The group's leader brings along a trusted companion. The group runs into alien animals and develops terrible allergies before they finally reach their destination, which is a real gem of a city.

THE MYSTERY

Where does the road end and what is the name of the leader's companion?

THE CLUES

You won't find the city on any map.

The companion sometimes walks and is sometimes carried in a basket.

The companion has four legs.

The road is made of yellow bricks.

CASE 18 SOLUTION

The road ends at the Emerald City and the companion's name is Toto.

why?

DOES ANYONE LOVE LUCY?

Lucy is suffering from a dangerous disease. Her family decides that she should undergo an operation, but Lucy is not told about it. The operation will be performed by someone who has never operated on a human being before.

THE MYSTERY

Why isn't Lucy told about her operation and who operates on her?

THE CLUES

Lucy was adopted and her family loves her very much.

Lucy has a license, but it's not a driver's license.

The person who operates on Lucy has a medical degree but is not a medical doctor.

Lucy is the family's "best friend."

CASE 1 SOLUTION

*Lucy is a dog. A veterinary surgeon
operates on her.*

THE MYSTERY MOUSE

Zack is allergic to most animals and avoids them whenever he can. Nonetheless, he owns a small mouse. He spends several hours every day holding or stroking his mouse, even though he doesn't love it.

THE MYSTERY

Why isn't Zack allergic to his mouse?

THE CLUES

Zack does not keep his mouse in a cage.

Zack's mouse does not move unless he pushes it.

Zack's mouse does not eat or drink.

Zack's mouse has a nice pad.

CASE 2 SOLUTION

Zack isn't allergic to his mouse because it's a computer mouse.

why?

POISON IVY?

Ivy learns that an overweight man needs surgery. She is not a doctor, but she agrees to perform the procedure. She carefully removes the body parts from her patient, including several major organs. He does not die and Ivy does not get in trouble.

THE MYSTERY

Why is Ivy allowed to do this?

THE CLUES

Ivy does the surgery free of charge.

Ivy has a very steady hand and uses only tweezers.

If Ivy makes a mistake, she will hear a buzz.

The patient is a man named Sam.

CASE 3 SOLUTION

Ivy is playing the game Operation®.

THE BRUTAL BEATING

A small, defenseless animal stands quietly in the sunshine. Suddenly, it is pulled up into the air by a rope and hit over and over with sticks until its body is crushed. Although many witness this beating, no one is punished.

THE MYSTERY

Why did this action take place?

THE CLUES

The action took place at a party.

Those who hit the animal could not see it.

Those who hit the animal were children.

The animal was beaten for what was inside it.

CASE 4 SOLUTION

*The animal is a piñata being broken
open at a party.*

TERRIBLE TEA

George attends a party, where he quickly gulps down a large iced tea in under a minute before having to leave unexpectedly. He suffers no ill effects, but other people at the party who drink the iced tea are poisoned and become violently sick.

THE MYSTERY

Why did the other people become ill and why didn't George?

THE CLUES

All the iced teas were exactly the same, and everyone drank an equal amount.

The tea itself wasn't poisoned, but something else in the glass was.

The iced teas looked completely normal.

The poison was frozen.

CASE 5 SOLUTION

The ice in the drinks was poisoned;
George drank his iced tea before the ice melted.

THE INCREDIBLE ESCAPE

Jake is being chased by a buffalo stampede when he comes to a wide, deep river. To escape, he must cross the river, but there is no bridge and he has no boat. He cannot even swim. Nonetheless, he easily gets away and, although the river is full, he doesn't even get wet.

THE MYSTERY

Why is Jake able to cross the river and why don't the buffalo follow?

THE CLUES

Jake uses no equipment or tools to cross the river.

The buffalo are excellent swimmers.

The buffalo weigh over 1,000 pounds each, but Jake weighs only 100 pounds.

It is wintertime.

CASE 6 SOLUTION

Jake can cross the river because it is frozen;
the buffalo are too heavyy to follow.

THE REAL ESTATE CAPER

Nina and Maia are making a fortune in real estate. Even though Nina never breaks the law, she is sent to jail several times. Maia follows the same procedures as Nina with many of the same properties, but she never goes to jail.

THE MYSTERY

Why did Nina go to jail?

THE CLUES

Nina was sent to jail without a trial.

Nina never left her home when she went to jail. In fact, she never even got out of her chair.

All Nina needs is a good roll, not parole.

Nina did not collect $200 on her way to jail.

CASE 7 SOLUTION

Nina is playing Monopoly® and landed on the
square that says, "Go to Jail."

CASE 8

GONE WITHOUT A TRACE

Sue is a talented sculptor. She crafts beautiful pieces that weigh hundreds of pounds and carefully delivers them to her clients. Within 24 hours of delivery, every sculpture disappears. Sue does not seem to be upset by these disappearances.

THE MYSTERY

Why isn't Sue upset, and what happens to the sculptures?

THE CLUES

The sculptures haven't been stolen.

Sue must work quickly.

The sculptures may be heat or light sensitive.

The sculptures are clear and cold.

CASE 8 SOLUTION

*Sue is an ice sculptor;
her sculptures melt.*

A MATTER OF DEGREES

A man from Chicago puts on shorts and a tank top, then goes outside in the middle of winter. The wind is blowing and it's 30° outside, but the man is happy that he's not bundled up for the winter like the rest of the people in Chicago.

THE MYSTERY

Why can the man tolerate the weather, and what is he doing?

THE CLUES

The man is completely comfortable.

The man is far from his work and home.

Everyone else around the man is dressed as he is.

The man is on vacation.

CASE 9 SOLUTION

The man took a trip to a place where the temperature is 30° Celsius.

why?

THE BAFFLING CRASH

Bob and Ursula are talking while Bob drives their little two-seater sports car down a winding road. Bob has a seat belt on, but Ursula does not. Suddenly, a truck hits their car. Bob has two broken legs and a broken pelvis, but Ursula doesn't have a scratch. Ursula calls the police right away, but can't tell them where the accident happened.

THE MYSTERY

Why isn't Ursula injured and why doesn't she know where the accident occurred?

THE CLUES

There was equal damage on the driver's and passenger's side of the car.

Ursula was not wearing any special protection.

Ursula has good vision, but she never saw the truck coming.

Ursula could hear Bob, but she couldn't see him.

CASE 10 SOLUTION

Ursula was not in the car; she was talking to Bob on his cell phone.

FOOLISH JULES

Jules is the guest of honor at a party where he downs seven drinks in three hours. Despite warnings from his friends, he runs outside, hops into the bright red sports car parked in the driveway and drives away. Minutes later, he crashes into a tree and totals the car. The police test Jules's blood and find no alcohol.

THE MYSTERY

Why were the test results negative, and why did Jules have the accident?

THE CLUES

The test results were accurate, but Jules did break the law.

Jules' drink of choice is bubbly and probably gave him a sugar high.

The accident was on October 4, 2003. Jules was born on October 4, 1988.

Jules did not drink any alcohol at the party.

CASE 11 SOLUTION

Jules was drinking soda,
but he was only 15 years old and didn't
know how to drive.

A CASE OF PACE

An elderly woman goes for a nice, slow walk. Two young men in great shape are right behind her, sprinting toward her. No matter how fast they run, they do not catch up with the woman.

THE MYSTERY

Why can't the men catch up with the woman?

THE CLUES

The men are running as fast as they can.

The men always stay seven feet behind the woman.

All three people paid money to be where they are.

All three people are indoors.

CASE 12 SOLUTION

*All three people are
on treadmills in a gym.*

THE CAPTIVE COMPETITOR

Chip is an athlete who is never allowed to leave his home alone, even though he is middle aged. When he does get out, under strict supervision, thousands of people come to watch him compete. Chip is in excellent health and has no known mental problems. He is well cared for and never complains about his living arrangements.

THE MYSTERY

Why doesn't Chip complain and what is his profession?

THE CLUES

Chip is a professional, yet he earns no money for himself.

Chip follows his instincts when he competes.

Even if Chip wanted to complain about being kept on such a tight leash, he couldn't really say anything.

Chip loves to go to the racetrack.

CASE 13 SOLUTION

Chip is a greyhound and he competes in dog races.

THE PECULIAR PURSE SNATCHING

Emily is sitting in a chair reading a book when a man bursts into her room and snatches her purse from right in front of her. He carries no weapon, but Emily does not stop him. She reports the crime to the police, giving a description of her purse but no details about the man.

THE MYSTERY

Why didn't Emily stop the man?

THE CLUES

Emily did not know the man, but she knew he was breaking into her home.
Emily speaks only English, but her book was written in another language.
Emily's hands were busy at the time of the break-in.
Emily did not see the man.

CASE 14 SOLUTION

*Emily is blind and was reading
a book in Braille.*

why?

THE DOCTOR OF DOOM?

Dr. Cooper goes into surgery and immediately passes out. The operation is finished by the time he comes to. After a few days, he operates on a sick child. Even though the hospital knows that the child will die if Dr. Cooper passes out again, he is allowed to operate unsupervised.

THE MYSTERY

Why did Dr. Cooper pass out, and why is he trusted to perform the operation on the child?

THE CLUES

Dr. Cooper's operation on the sick child was a success.

It did not surprise anyone that Dr. Cooper passed out.

Dr. Cooper was not operating when he passed out.

Dr. Cooper was lying down when he passed out.

CASE 15 SOLUTION

Dr. Cooper passed out because he was given anesthesia; he can operate now that he is recovered from his surgery.

PETER'S PECULIAR PICTURES

In addition to pictures of his wife and children, Peter carries pictures of dead people with him at all times. Peter admires the people, but they are not members of his family. Even though some of the pictures are very valuable, Peter often gives the pictures away.

THE MYSTERY

Why does Peter carry the pictures and why does he give them away?

THE CLUES

The fewer pictures Peter gives away, the better he feels.

The pictures are wallet-sized.

Peter trades the pictures for things that he wants.

Peter's favorite picture is a green portrait of Benjamin Franklin.

CASE 16 SOLUTION

Peter carries the pictures because they are money, which he exchanges for the things he buys.

why?

A FRIGHTENING FALL

Connie hugs her children tightly and kisses them goodbye. As she steps out the door, she falls and screams. Her children watch in horror as she flails about, but they do nothing to help her. Within an hour, they are all one big happy family again and talk about the fall over lunch.

THE MYSTERY

Why did Connie fall and why didn't the children help her?

THE CLUES

Connie wasn't hurt by the fall.

The children couldn't have reached their mom even if they wanted to.

Connie fell thousands of feet, but had a soft landing.

The door Connie walked through was on an airplane.

CASE 17 SOLUTION

Connie jumped out of a plane.
The children didn't help because
she had a parachute.

why?

THE UNTOUCHED ICE CREAM

An ice cream stand offers free giant sundaes at sunset during the summer. At the end of the summer, the owner reviews his records and finds that, even though he had many customers, not one sundae was given away. He is not surprised.

THE MYSTERY

Why doesn't the owner ever have to give away any sundaes?

THE CLUES

The customers laughed when they read the offer.

The ice cream stand is in Alaska.

In 20 years of business, the owner has never given away a sundae. And he never will.

The ice cream stand only makes this offer during the summer, when the days are very long.

CASE 18 SOLUTION

The owner never has to give away any sundaes because the sun never sets in Alaska during the summer months.

ABOUT THE AUTHOR

Bob Moog, co-founder of University Games and publisher of Spinner Books, has been creating games and puzzles and the like since childhood. He tormented his four younger siblings with quizzes, conundrums and physical and mental challenges during the 1960s. Now, he introduces the Spinner Books for Kids™ series, hoping it will challenge and puzzle you as much as his early "work" did his family 40 years ago.

Moog is the author of several other puzzle/game and children's books, including *Gummy Bear Goes to Camp*, *Kids Battle the Grown-Ups*™, *Totally Gross!*™ and *Secret Identities*™.

Enjoy Spinner Books?

30 SECOND MYSTERIES FOR KIDS
Follow the clues to crack the case!

Kids Battle the **Grown-Ups**
Who really knows more...the kids or the grown-ups?

new edition! **20 Questions** for kids
play the classic game of people, places and things!
ages 7 to 12 — for 2 to 10 players

TOTALLY GROSS! THE GAME of Science

Get the Original Games!

Find these games and more at your nearest toy store.

AreYouGame.com

UNIVERSITY **G**AMES

© 2004 University Games Corporation 2030 Harrison St., San Francisco, CA 94110
1-800-347-4818 www.ugames.com